The Boostertron

by Rob Alcraft
Illustrated by Bill Ledge

OXFORD
UNIVERSITY PRESS

In this story ...

Cam

Cam can turn into different animals.

Jin

Ben

Mr Trainer
(teacher)

Mrs Butterworth
(cook)

Jin, Ben and Cam had made a Boostertron.
"It will make our powers stronger," Cam said.
"Do not test it until I get back," Mr Trainer said.
He left to check on the next group.

"I cannot wait to test the Boostertron!" said Jin. In his excitement, he hit one of the keys.

It was too late. The power beam hit Cam and she became an elephant.
"Oh, no!" said Ben.

Cam needed to get back to normal, but she was stuck as an elephant! Cam started to panic.

"The Boostertron will turn her back," said Jin.
The boys hit the keys.

Cam did not like the Boostertron. She needed to escape. Cam burst out of the wall. She left a huge, elephant-sized hole.

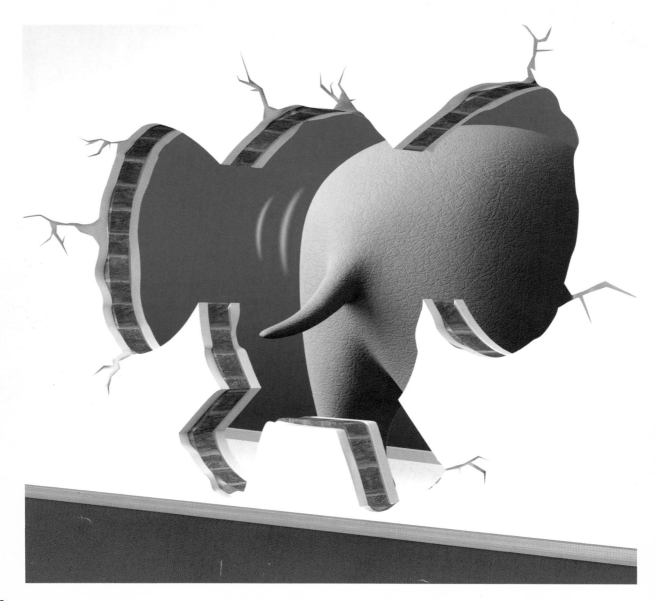

"Stop, Cam!" Ben shouted. "Come back here!"
Cam did not stop.

Cam made a new hole.
"We must stop her!" Jin shouted.

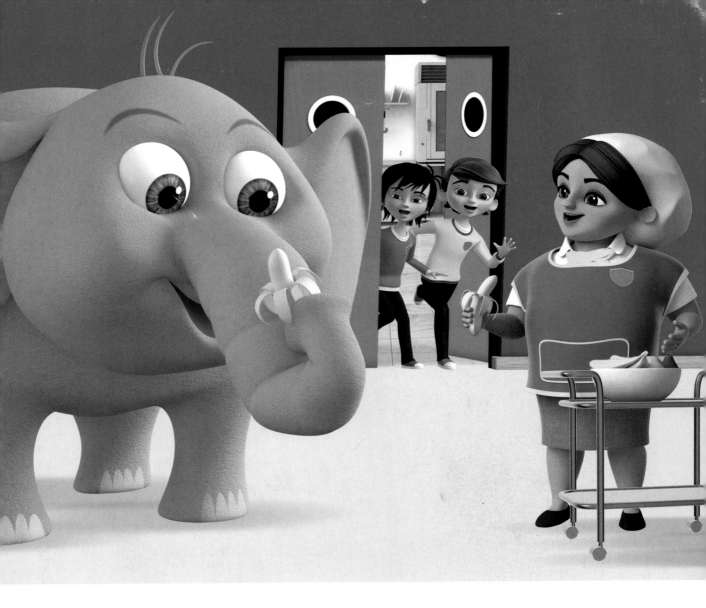

The boys ran to the dinner hall.
When they got there, they saw Mrs Butterworth.
"I gave her a banana from the trolley to make
her stop," said Mrs Butterworth.

Jin held up a few extra bananas. "Look at these, Cam!" he said.
Jin led her back to the classroom.

Just then, Mr Trainer came in.

"Did you test the Boostertron?" he asked.

Jin nodded. "I did not mean to get Cam with the power beam," he said.

"I said not to use the Boostertron until I was here," Mr Trainer said.

Jin felt bad. "Next time, I will wait," he replied.

Mr Trainer hit a key on the Boostertron. *ZAP!*
Cam was back to normal. "Phew!" she said.
"I am glad to be back."

Retell the story ...

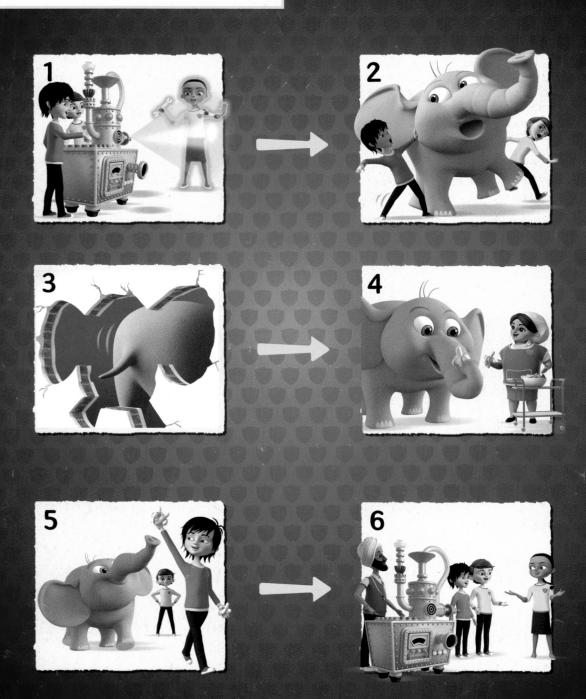